WELCOME SPEECHES AND RESPONSES FOR ALL OCCASIONS

Abingdon Press
Nashville

WELCOME SPEECHES AND RESPONSES FOR ALL OCCASIONS

Copyright © 1992 by Abingdon Press

97 98 99 00 01 02—10 9

ISBN 0-687-44307-5

ACKNOWLEDGMENTS

Welcome addresses on pages 10, 11, 12, and 13 are by Carol Overton. Used by permission.
Homecoming/Church Anniversary on pages 21-22 is by Faye Lyons. Used by permission.
Homecoming/Memorial Service on pages 23-24 is by Faye Lyons. Used by permission. Portions adapted from *Handbook of the Christian Year,* ed. Hoyt Hickman, Don Saliers, Laurence Stookey, and James White. Copyright © 1986 by Abingdon Press. Reprinted by permission.
Mother's Day Tribute to Motherhood on page 28 is by Iris R. Jones-Gboizo. Used by permission.
Father's Day Welcome is adapted from *Services for National Days.* Copyright © 1991 by Abingdon Press.
"Listen, Lord (A Prayer)" is from *God's Trombones* by James Weldon Johnson. Copyright 1927 The Viking Press, Inc. © renewed 1955 by Grace Nail Johnson. Used by permission of Viking Penguin, a division of Penguin Books USA Inc.
Mother's Day and Memories on page 50 is by Iris R. Jones-Gboizo. Used by permission.
Joy (A Single Mother's Prayer of Thanksgiving) on page 51 is by Iris R. Jones-Gboizo. Used by permission.
"Children's Day," "What Rally Should Mean," "Building Bridges," "When Christmas Comes," "A Greeting," and "A Christmastide Thought" are from *Eureka Plan and Program Book for All Occasions* by Mattie B. Shannon. Copyright © renewal 1962 by Mattie B. Shannon. Reprinted by permission.

Scripture quotations, except for brief paraphrases, are from the King James or Authorized version of the Bible.

CONTENTS

INTRODUCTION

If you are asked to give a welcome speech, do so willingly, knowing that God will be with you and help you. Remember that the purpose of a welcome speech is to make guests and members alike feel at home in your church, God's house. The length and even the words you choose will not be as important as your sincerity and warmth.

This book includes sample welcome speeches and responses you can adapt to your own church. It also has a section of poetry and some familiar scriptures appropriate to special days for your use in writing your own speeches. The scripture passages are taken from the King James Version of the Bible.

SOME GENERAL WORDS
OF WELCOME

A WELCOME FROM THE PASTOR

Honored guests _____(names)_____ , on behalf of my staff and other officials, I bring you these words of welcome. We are glad you responded to our invitation. We hope your stay will be a rewarding one. Welcome!

WELCOME

We are honored beyond words to have this opportunity to extend words of welcome here today. We are elated to welcome you, knowing the purpose you represent. To say "You are welcome" is our way of letting you know just how glad we are to have you with us. We do want you to feel at home and that you are among friends. We welcome you here, for we feel you are going to be a blessing to us during your stay. We want you to enjoy yourself in our church home. We hope this occasion will be in your memory for many years to come. Welcome!

WELCOME

W hen God calls all of us together
E ach of us must show
L ove to our guests. So Let's
C ome together and enjoy
O urselves, open our hearts, and
M ake each one feel
E specially Welcome!

WELCOME

Welcome is a word we do not say lightly; it is spoken from hearts of sincerity. We welcome you gladly into God's house; with arms open wide we welcome you just as God does. Welcome!

WELCOME

Honored guests _____(names)_____ , we
are honored to bring you words of welcome today. We
feel blessed to share this occasion with you. We thank
God for this day. We know we are going to have a good
time just because you are here. So we hope you enjoy
this program and make yourself at home. Just as you
would feel free in your own house of worship, feel free
in our church to praise God and lift your hand to his
word. Welcome!

A GENERAL RESPONSE

I thank you, (Sister/Brother) _____,
for that beautiful welcome. I am _____
and have been chosen to respond to the welcome. On
behalf of my pastor, other pastors (names if known),
and all guests present, I accept your heartfelt welcome.
Thank you.

WELCOME SPEECHES AND RESPONSES FOR SPECIFIC DAYS AND OCCASIONS

PASTOR ANNIVERSARY/APPRECIATION

Welcome

Honored guests, Pastor (guest preacher), choirs (list), (other special guests), and our pastor's family. I am glad to be here today to welcome you to our day of appreciation for Pastor _____. This is a day of celebration for what the Lord has done in the life of God's people and especially through the life of Pastor _____, God's undershepherd.

We are all ambassadors for Christ, but most especially Pastor _____, who represents Christ in the affairs of the Kingdom on earth. The task of a preacher is not an easy one, and the responsibilities are large. For this reason, we also want to say a special word of appreciation to our pastor's family.

Jeremiah 3:15 states, "I will give you pastors according to mine heart, which shall feed you with knowledge and understanding." Again, I say "welcome" to you who have joined us to honor the one who so faithfully feeds this flock.

Response

I thank you, (Sister/Brother) _____, for that beautiful welcome. I am _____ and have been chosen to respond to the welcome. In Matthew 10:41 we read, "He that receiveth a prophet in the name of a prophet shall receive a prophet's reward; and he that receiveth a righteous man in the name of a righteous man shall receive a righteous man's reward." We are honored to be here today to praise this righteous individual, Pastor _____, and on behalf of my pastor and all other pastors and churches present, I accept your heartfelt welcome. Thank you.

CHOIR ANNIVERSARY/APPRECIATION

Welcome

Honored guests (here welcome should be extended to the guest preacher and choir, musicians, soloists, and visitors who are present. If charter members of the choir are present, they should be recognized), it is my privilege to extend to you a welcome to our ____th anniversary for the _____ choir. The psalmist has said, "Make a joyful noise unto the Lord, all ye lands. Serve the Lord with gladness: come before his presence with singing" (Ps. 100:1-2). A Choir Day celebration is one where we, the people of God, take our harps off the willows and sing the Lord's song! With that in mind, I bid you welcome to this day of celebration and song.

Response

What an honor it is to be here today and to sing with you that Wondrous Story! Thank you, (Sister/

Brother) _____, for that welcoming speech and for reminding us that from our earliest history the Lord has called on us to sing a new song. In I Chronicles we find David speaking to the high priestly order: "David spake to the chief of the Levites to appoint their brethren to be the singers with instruments of music, psalteries and harps and cymbals, sounding, by lifting up the voice with joy" (I Chron. 15:16). It is our privilege to lift our voices with yours, and on behalf of all gathered here today I accept your welcome.

HOMECOMING/CHURCH ANNIVERSARY

Pastor, fellow parishioners, guests, I am happy to be here today, celebrating with all of you this our ____ th anniversary. At this time in our service, we pause to honor members in our midst who have been with us the longest and shortest periods of time.

_____ joined _____ in _____ under the pastorate of _____. (She/He) is truly a pioneer of our church and has been faithful through the years, giving generously of (herself/himself). We are sorry (she/he) could not be here today, but we know (his/her) thoughts and prayers are with us. It is a special blessing and honor to be on the membership roll since _____. We are blessed to have one of our own who has endured for so long. I am sure that if (she/he) could have come today (she/he) might have quoted II Timothy 4:7: "I have fought a good fight, I have finished my course, I have kept the faith."

_____ on _____, 19____, became our youngest member on roll. _____ is being shaped and molded by those of us around (her/him).

Proverbs 20:7 reads: "The just man walketh in his integrity: his children are blessed after him." Let us nurture (her/him) with love, care, and faith in God, for (she/he) is an important part of our future.

Let Us Pray:

Our heavenly Father, we thank thee for the great blessing of thy loving presence with our church across the changing years and pray you will continue to be with us throughout the years to come. We are grateful for members, young and old, who sacrifice their time and talent for the growth of our church. May their Christian service be a beacon for all to follow. Guide and direct us into rewarding years ahead. These mercies we ask in the name of thy Son, Jesus, our Lord and Savior. *Amen.*

HOMECOMING/MEMORIAL SERVICE

With bowed heads and humble hearts, we recognize,

God of all holiness, that
you gave our saints different gifts on earth
but one holy city in heaven.
Give us grace to follow their good example,
that we may know the joy you have prepared
for all who love you;
through your Son Jesus Christ our Lord.

                                        Amen.

This is a special moment in our homecoming activities when we pause in remembrance of loved ones who have fought the good fight, have finished the race, and have kept the faith. Since our last homecoming celebration these honored and remembered today have answered God's call from their labors and welcomed those long-awaited words: "Well done thou good and faithful servant. You have been faithful over a few things; come on up high, and I will make you ruler over many!"

O God of both the living and the dead, we praise your holy name for all your servants who have finished their course in faith. . . . Especially (here the names may be given). We pray that, encouraged by their example, we may be partakers with them of the inheritance of the saints in light; through the merits of your Son Jesus Christ our Lord. Amen.

CHILDREN'S DAY

Welcome

Honored guests, Pastor _____, all visitors, and our children:

> Children's Day! Most loved of all
> In every childish heart;
> It brings to mind a Savior's call
> And blessed memories start;
> We see the Christ of Galilee
> With hand on tiny head—
> "O let the children come to me,"
> The Savior sweetly said.

> Children's Day! O may we keep
> This festival of our own
> With pledge so solemn and so deep
> To reach the Father's throne:
> May we resolve in earnest way
> To give the Christ our all;

We hear the words of olden day—
We'll heed the loving call.

Children's Day! The happy time
When joyous carols ring,
For childish tongues in notes sublime
Bring praise to Christ the King;
The children in the temple old
Once sweetly praised the Christ;
His face we may not now behold
But we have his words unpriced.

And it is in the name of Christ, who came to us as a little child, that I welcome you to this special service.

Response

Thank you, (Sister/Brother) _____, for that beautiful welcome (the welcome may have been given by a child; in that case, be sure to recognize the giver). My name is _____, and I have been chosen to respond to the welcome. In the name of Christ, who took little children into his arms and blessed them, and on behalf of all children and guests gathered here today, I accept your heartfelt welcome. Thank you.

FAMILY DAY

Welcome

Honored guests _____, as I look out across the families gathered here today, some with three generations, many with fewer, but still *family,* I am thankful that God ordained the family to be a shelter for love and fulfillment so that none of us, his children, should be lonely. Of course there is loneliness present today, and we remember those who are not with us for any reason and those who have departed from the earth. Still, we rejoice that wherever our loved ones are, our loving heavenly Father is their parent as well and that we all belong to his family. It is in that certitude that I welcome you to this day of celebration.

Response

Thank you, (Sister/Brother) _____, for reminding us that God is our parent. Let us always remember "what manner of love the Father hath bestowed upon us, that we should be called the [children] of God" (I John 3:1). It is as your (Sister/Brother) that I accept your kind welcome in the name of this great family. Thank you.

MOTHER'S DAY TRIBUTE TO MOTHERHOOD

Today is Mother's Day. It is a day to give honor and recognition to our mothers, and to those who are just like mothers to us. It is a day to thank them for their love, and care, and support throughout the years.

Mothers are special. They wipe runny noses, bandage scraped knees, and dry away tears. They fix broken toys, drive us everywhere we need to go, and still have time to make our favorite treat.

Mothers are special. They cried when we went off to college, and they even cried when we graduated. They cried when we got married, cried when we had our first child, and cried when we had to leave after a holiday visit.

Mothers are special. We take them wherever they need to go, thread the needle for them, and make sure that someone is always nearby. We do the scrubbing, the shopping, and the dishes, and show them how to work the remote control.

On this special day, we honor all mothers—whether they are our biological or spiritual mother.

FATHER'S DAY

Welcome

Honored guests, Pastor _____ (list any visiting pastors or churches), and all fathers present, welcome to our service of celebration on this Father's Day. This day we honor those fathers who taught us skills and tenderness, played with us and worked for us, loved us and advised us. Today we say thanks to those fathers who worked to provide more than shelter, who provided a home for their children. Today we honor those fathers who came with their families to church, instead of dropping them off. Today we celebrate those fathers whose love for their children is modeled on God's love for all children. Today we thank God for loving fathers, and for all those men, though not our biological fathers, who have cared for us. Welcome.

Response

Thank you, (Sister/Brother) _____, for those inspiring words. In Ephesians we read, "Honour thy father and mother; which is the first commandment with promise; that it may be well with thee, and thou mayest live long on the earth. And, ye fathers, provoke not your children to wrath: but bring them up in the nurture and admonition of the Lord" (Eph. 6:2-4). We are glad to be here to honor those men who nurture this church, and on behalf of those men and all gathered here I accept your welcome.

MEN'S DAY

Welcome

Honored guests _____, I am delighted to welcome our special guests and to extend words of welcome to all men here today. Every man here is outstanding; not perhaps by the world's standards, but by God's standards of love and service. It is to honor these many outstanding individuals that I say to you, welcome!

Response

Thank you, (Sister/Brother) _____, for those inspiring words. Genesis tells us that "the Lord God formed man of the dust of the ground, and breathed into his nostrils the breath of life; and man became a living soul" (Gen. 2:7). Our very souls are delighted to be here at this celebration today, and on behalf of all guests, I accept your warm words of welcome. Thank you.

WOMEN'S DAY

Welcome

Honored guests, from the very beginning of time, from Eve, the mother of all living, to the present day, women have played a significant role in the life of the church. Today we honor and applaud the women of _____ church, without whom, it is safe to say, there would be no church! Proverbs 31:10 states, "Who can find a virtuous woman? for her price is far above rubies." The "rubies" set in the crown of this church, the Mother's Board, the Deaconesses, the Missionary societies and auxiliaries (list any groups that are part of your church or denomination) all glow as reminders that God has blessed us. It is in the name of these women, and all women, that I bid you welcome to this celebration of Women's Day.

Response

Thank you, (Sister/Brother) _____, for that inspired welcome. Not only do we trace our heritage back to Eve, the mother of all living, but we read in Galatians, "When the fulness of the time was come, God sent forth his Son, *made of a woman,* made under the law, To redeem them that were under the law, that we might receive the adoption of sons" (Gal. 4:4-5 emphasis added). It was through a woman that the Son of God came to earth, and it is in his name that I accept your welcome to this day of celebration.

MISSIONS

Foreign Missions Day

Welcome

Honored guests _____, we are mindful of the Bible's admonition to go and teach all nations and of the precious promise of Christ's presence with all who go in his name to serve in foreign fields. I bid you welcome here today so that together we may all give thanks to God for the wondrous blessings of peace in our hearts and, ultimately, in the world. Welcome.

Home Missions Day

Welcome

Honored guests _____, even as we count the abundance of God's goodness to us, we are aware that there are others in our area who lack food, clothing, and adequate shelter. We are gathered here today with sharing hearts and outstretched hands to serve God through our home missions. It is in the name of the one who opens our eyes to our opportunities for Christian service near our homes, that I say to you, welcome.

USHER BOARD ANNIVERSARY/APPRECIATION

Welcome

Honored guests (here include any visiting ushers, older members who have served faithfully, and charter members of the usher board), we are assembled here today to pay tribute to our doorkeepers. Most usher boards have as their special verse Psalm 84:10: "For a day in thy courts is better than a thousand. I had rather be a doorkeeper in the house of my God, than to dwell in the tents of wickedness."

We wish for our own usher board a thousand days in the house of God. Truly, our doorkeepers open more than just the doors; they open the opportunity for the unsaved to be saved, the downtrodden to be lifted up, and the weary to find rest. I welcome you to this day of celebration as we appreciate and applaud the ministry of our ushers.

Response

Truly, the presence of the Lord is in this place! Thank you, (Sister/Brother) _____, for that inspiring welcome. It is our pleasure and privilege to join you on this day to praise the Lord for his servants. On behalf of my pastor, Pastor _____, the visiting ushers, and all other guests I accept your heartfelt welcome.

GRADUATE RECOGNITION DAY

Welcome

Honored guests _____, and our graduates, I am glad to be here today and to have been chosen to extend our welcome to you. As I stand here I remember my own graduation day with all its hopes and fears. Graduation is a time to dream dreams about the future. In I Corinthians we read, "When I was a child, I spake as a child, I understood as a child, I thought as a child: but when I became a man, I put away childish things. For now we see through a glass, darkly; but then face to face: now I know in part; but then shall I know even as also I am known" (I Cor. 13:11-12). Today our graduates stand ready to put away their childish things, and we are ready to stand with them and encourage them as they seek to know all things more clearly. It is in that spirit that I welcome you to this day of celebration.

Response

Thank you, (Sister/Brother) _____, for those uplifting words. On behalf of all gathered here today, I accept your welcome as we remember that the hope of our future is our children, and especially those we honor at this graduation celebration.

MEMORIAL DAY

Welcome

Honored guests _____, so many memories come to us today, so many lives are remembered. Down through the ages, in war after war, millions have sacrificed their lives for the causes of freedom. As we remember them today, we remember their sacrifice and thank God for their precious gift. Here in this house of worship we also remember another sacrifice. The sacrifice of Christ on the cross, a sacrifice that brought the greatest hope and freedom to the world. This place is the gathering space for the people of the Resurrection. Our memories are joyful because we know that Christ has conquered death. It is in that certain knowledge that I welcome you to this time of remembrance.

Response

Thank you, (Sister/Brother) _____, for those words. Our Lord has said, "Blessed are those who mourn, for they shall be comforted." We have a great promise—that our loved ones are in the loving care of God and that we will join them one day for a great reunion. It is in looking forward to that reunion that I say, on behalf of all those gathered here, thank you for your words of welcome.

MARTIN LUTHER KING, JR., DAY

Welcome

Honored guests, _____, I am humbled and grateful to have been chosen to extend to you our welcome as we gather once again to recognize and remember that great American, Martin Luther King, Jr. All of us remember Dr. King as a man who dreamed dreams, but beyond that he was a preacher, a prophet, and a pastor. In Ephesians we read,

> Finally, my brethren, be strong in the Lord, and in the power of his might. . . . take unto you the whole armour of God. . . . Stand therefore, having your loins girt about with truth, and having on the breastplate of righteousness; And your feet shod with the preparation of the gospel of peace; Above all, taking the shield of faith, wherewith ye shall be able to quench all the fiery darts of the wicked. And take the helmet of salvation, and the sword of the Spirit, which is the word of God: Praying always with all prayer and supplication in the Spirit, and watching thereunto with all perseverance and supplication for all saints.
>
> (Eph. 6:10-18)

Our themes for today are love, justice, and liberation, not just for African American people, but for all people. It is in that spirit that I bid you welcome to this service of celebration.

Response

Thank you, (Sister/Brother)_____, for those inspired words. George Santayana was correct when he said, "Those who cannot remember the past are condemned to repeat it." We must always remember the legacy Dr. King left, and it is in recognition of that legacy that I accept your welcome. Thank you.

POETRY, PRAYERS, AND SCRIPTURE

RING OUT, WILD BELLS

Ring out, wild bells, to the wild sky,
  The flying cloud, the frosty light:
  The year is dying in the night;
Ring out, wild bells, and let him die.

Ring out the old, ring in the new,
  Ring, happy bells, across the snow:
  The year is going, let him go;
Ring out the false, ring in the true.

Ring out the grief that saps the mind,
  For those that here we see no more;
  Ring out the feud of rich and poor,
Ring in redress to all mankind.

.   .   .   .

Ring out false pride in place and blood,
  The civic slander and the spite;
  Ring in the love of truth and right,
Ring in the common love of good.

.   .   .   .

Ring in the valiant man and free,
  The larger heart, the kindlier hand;
  Ring out the darkness of the land,
Ring in the Christ that is to be.

  —*Alfred Tennyson*

BROTHERHOOD

What might be done if men were wise,
What glorious deeds, my suffering brother,
   Would they unite
   In love and right,
And cease their scorn of one another?

Oppression's heart might be imbued
With kindling drops of loving-kindness,
   And knowledge pour
   From shore to shore
Light on the eyes of mental blindness.

All slavery, warfare, lies, and wrongs,
All vice and crime, might die together;
   And meat and corn,
   To each man born,
Be free as warmth in summer weather.

The meanest wretch that ever trod,
The deepest sunk in guilt and sorrow,

Might stand erect
In self-respect
And share the teeming world tomorrow.

What might be done? This might be done,
And more than this, my suffering brother,
More than the tongue
E'er said or sung,
If men were wise and loved each other.
—*Charles Mackay*
(*Reprinted*)

LISTEN, LORD (A PRAYER)

O Lord, we come this morning knee-bowed and body-bent before thy throne of grace. O Lord—this morning—bow our hearts beneath our knees, and our knees in some lonesome valley. We come this morning like empty pitchers to a full fountain, with no merits of our own. O Lord, open up a window of heaven, and lean out far over the battlements of glory, and listen this morning, Amen.

—*James Weldon Johnson*

STANZAS ON FREEDOM

Men! whose boast it is that ye
Come of fathers brave and free,
If there breathe on earth a slave,
Are ye truly free and brave?
If ye do not feel the chain
When it works a brother's pain,
Are ye not base slaves indeed,
Slaves unworthy to be freed!

Is true Freedom but to break
Fetters for our own dear sake,
And, with leathern hearts, forget
That we owe mankind a debt?
No! True Freedom is to share
All the chains our brothers wear,
And, with heart and hand, to be
Earnest to make others free!

They are slaves who fear to speak
For the fallen and the weak;

They are slaves who will not choose
Hatred, scoffing and abuse,
Rather than in silence shrink
From the truth they needs must think:
They are slaves who dare not be
In the right with two or three.
                    —*James Russell Lowell*

WISE COUNSEL

I am not bound to win, but I am bound to be true. I am not bound to succeed, but I am bound to live up to what light I have. I must stand with anybody that stands right; stand with him while he is right and part with him when he goes wrong.

I desire so to conduct the affairs of this administration that if at the end, when I come to lay down the reins of power, I have lost every other friend on earth, I shall at least have one friend left, and that friend shall be down inside me.

I have been driven many times to my knees, by the overwhelming conviction that I had nowhere else to go. My own wisdom, and that of all about me, seemed insufficient for that day.

—*Abraham Lincoln*

MOTHER'S DAY AND MEMORIES

Today is Mother's Day. For some, it is a day to remember all the joys of mothering. For others, it is a time to celebrate the birth of your brand new baby boy or girl. For those who are new mothers, it might be nice to recall your pregnancy. Do you remember trying to get comfortable in bed? A pillow here, and here, and there? Do you remember the charley horse you got each morning, just when you were about to get up?

Perhaps you remember the nightly acrobatics your little one made when you were just about to doze off. Do you remember the acne you got, and all the bottles of baby oil and vitamin E you bought so that the stretch marks would go away?

But Mother's Day is also a day to honor the woman who birthed us. It's a day to let her know how grateful we are that she put up with us—to let her know how much we appreciate her love and care. Mother's Day was intended to be a day of more than just candy and flowers and cards. It was meant to be a day to celebrate mother love.

The heart of every family is the mother. So as we celebrate today, let us remember all mothers—whether yours or somebody else's. Let us remember those mothers who have died, and honor those who live. May we also honor those who have been just like a mother to us, and also encourage those who have just embarked on this journey of love.

JOY

(A Single Mother's Prayer of Thanksgiving)

Lord, I thank you for your church
I thank you for the smiles that greet us as we enter
Thank you for the patience you give to those
　　who gracefully sit through services when my child is
　　restless
For those who always encourage me to keep bringing
　　him.

Thank you for my call to service
　　to serve your people and your church
Thank you for strengthening me even when I feel I
　　cannot go on
Thank you for all the unexpected blessings
And for all the joy you bring.

Amen.

WHAT RALLY SHOULD MEAN

"To assemble together for action true,—"
I think that's what rally should mean;
Not merely to plan but to see it through,—
Thus purpose sincere is seen;
Assemble we must with prayer and with praise
That souls be in tune with God's plan;
Then together we'll work through the coming days
To serve Christ as best we can.

O this is the meaning of rally sincere,—
'Tis prayer, praise and pledging to serve;
Together for action we gather here,
From duty we must not swerve;
With Jesus the Lord as our Counsel and Guide,
O forward we'll go from this hour,
Determined to serve Him whatever betide,
Endued with our Savior's power.

BUILDING BRIDGES

An old man going a lone highway
Came at evening cold and gray,
To a chasm vast and deep and wide
Without a bridge to span the tide;
The old man crossed in twilight dim,
The sullen stream held no fear for him.
He turned when on the other side
And built a bridge to span the tide.

"Old man," said a pilgrim near,
"You waste your strength with building here.
Your journey ends with ending day.
You ne'er again will pass this way.
Your feet no more must need pass o'er
This sullen stream with sullen roar.
You've crossed the chasm deep and wide.
Why build this bridge at eventide?"

The old man turned his hoary head.
"Friend, in the path I've come," he said,
"There followeth after me today
A youth whose feet must pass this way.
This chasm that's as naught to me
To that fair youth may a pitfall be.
He, too, must cross in twilight dim—
Good friend, I build the bridge for him."

—Selected.
(Reprinted in Methodist Protestant-Recorder)

WHEN CHRISTMAS COMES

When Christmas comes a different earth
Seems filled with deeds of kindly love,
And grateful souls recall the birth
Of Christ Who came from God above.
A flame of mystic light is found
And songs of holy joy abound,
A message wings the world around
When Christmas comes.

When Christmas comes we see our need
And open hands their bounty share;
A peace that came with Christ indeed
Now reigns with shining wings and fair;
Our hearts forget the ways of strife,
In memories of a Saviour's life,
And every soul with hope is rife,
When Christmas comes.

FOOTPRINTS

One night I had a dream—
I dreamed I was walking along the beach
   with the Lord and
Across the sky flashed scenes of my life.
For each scene I noticed two sets of
   footprints in the sand.
One belonged to me and the other to the Lord.
When the last scene of my life flashed before me,
I looked back at the footprints in the sand.
I noticed that many times along the
   path of my life,
There was only one set of footprints.
I also noticed that it happened at the
   very lowest and saddest times in my life.
This really bothered me and I questioned
   the Lord about it.
"Lord, you said that once I decided
   to follow you,
You would walk with me all the way.
But I have noticed that during the most

troublesome times in my life,
There is only one set of footprints.
I don't understand why in times when I
    needed you the most, you would leave me."
The Lord replied, "My precious child,
    I love you and I would never, never leave you
    during your times of trial and suffering.
When you saw only one set of footprints,
It was then that I carried you."

—*Author Unknown*

THE DAY AND THE WORK

To each man is given a day and his work for the day;
And once, and no more, he is given to travel this way.
And woe if he flies from the task, whatever the odds;
For the task is appointed to him on the scroll of the gods.

There is waiting a work where only his hands can avail;
And so, if he falters, a chord in the music will fail.
He may laugh to the sky, he may lie for an hour in the sun;
But he dare not go hence till the labor appointed is done.

To each man is given a marble to carve for the wall;
A stone that is needed to heighten the beauty of all;
And only his soul has the magic to give it a grace;
And only his hand has the cunning to give it a place.

.   .   .   .

Yes, the task that is given to each man, no other can do;
So the errand is waiting; it has waited through ages for you.
And now you appear; and the hushed ones are turning
    their gaze,
To see what you do with your chance in the chamber
    of days.

—*Edwin Markham*

A GREETING

Here I have come with a bright, happy greeting,—
Christmas, glad Christmas is here;
'Tis a welcome, sweet welcome I'm truly repeating
With a wish that is also sincere;—
I hope Christmas brings you a happiness true.
To last every day of the long year through.

A CHRISTMASTIDE THOUGHT

O have you received a blest Christmastide thought
In the story of Wise Men of old,
Who ceaselessly, faithfully Jesus sought
That their eyes might the King behold;
A wonderful star in the bright heavens gleamed—
Its glory was holy and free;
O God's light would lead them through ways they had
    dreamed,
Where the King in His beauty would be.

O sometimes at Christmas the clear heavens shine
And my faith is a beautiful star;
I know that their journey will truly be mine
Though it lead through the lands afar;
And lo, there's a hope that to me is so plain,—
I know I shall find my reward;
As the search for the Sages was not in vain,
I, too, shall see Jesus the Lord!

SCRIPTURE

But as for me and my house, we will serve the Lord. (Josh. 24:15)

For there is hope of a tree, if it be cut down, that it will sprout again, and that the tender branch thereof will not cease. Though the root thereof wax old in the earth, and the stock thereof die in the ground; Yet through the scent of water it will bud, and bring forth boughs like a plant. (Job 14:7-9)

The lines are fallen unto me in pleasant places; yea, I have a goodly heritage. (Ps. 16:6)

Let the words of my mouth, and the meditation of my heart, be acceptable in thy sight, O Lord, my strength, and my redeemer. (Ps. 19:14)

Delight thyself also in the Lord; and he shall give thee the desires of thine heart. (Ps. 37:4)

My heart is fixed, O God, my heart is fixed: I will sing and give praise. (Ps. 57:7)

Make a joyful noise unto God, all ye lands: Sing forth the honour of his name: make his praise glorious. (Ps. 66:1-2)

How amiable are thy tabernacles, O Lord of hosts! (Ps. 84:1)

Blessed are they that dwell in thy house: they will be still praising thee. (Ps. 84:4)

For a day in thy courts is better than a thousand. I had rather be a doorkeeper in the house of my God, than to dwell in the tents of wickedness. (Ps. 84:10)

Lord, thou hast been our dwelling place in all generations. Before the mountains were brought forth, or ever thou hadst formed the earth and the world, even from everlasting to everlasting, thou art God. (Ps. 90:1-2)

Make a joyful noise unto the Lord, all the earth: make a loud noise, and rejoice, and sing praise. (Ps. 98:4)

I remember the days of old; I meditate on all thy works; I muse on the work of thy hands. (Ps. 143:5)

In all thy ways acknowledge him, and he shall direct thy paths. (Prov. 3:6)

A man that hath friends must shew himself friendly and there is a friend that sticketh closer than a brother. (Prov. 18:24)

Strength and honour are her clothing; and she shall rejoice in time to come. (Prov. 31:25)

She openeth her mouth with wisdom; and in her tongue is the law of kindness. (Prov. 31:26)

Her children arise up, and call her blessed; her husband also, and he praiseth her. (Prov. 31:28)

Two are better than one; because they have a good reward for their labour. For if they fall, the one will lift up his fellow: but woe to him that is alone when he falleth; for he hath not another to help him up. (Eccles. 4:9-10)

I returned, and saw under the sun, that the race is not to the swift, nor the battle to the strong, neither yet bread to the wise, nor yet riches to men of understanding, nor yet favour to men of skill; but time and chance happeneth to them all. (Eccles. 9:11)

Remember now thy Creator in the days of thy youth, while the evil days come not, nor the years draw nigh, when thou shalt say, I have no pleasure in them. (Eccles. 12:1)

The wolf also shall dwell with the lamb, and the leopard shall lie down with the kid; and the calf and the young lion and the fatling together; and a little child shall lead them. (Isa. 11:6)

They helped every one his neighbour; and every one said to his brother, Be of good courage. (Isa. 41:6)

Ye are the light of the world. A city that is set on an hill cannot be hid. Neither do men light a candle, and put it under a bushel, but on a candlestick; and it giveth light unto all that are in the house. Let your light so shine before men, that they may see your good works, and glorify your Father which is in heaven. (Matt. 5:14-16)

The harvest truly is plenteous, but the labourers are few; Pray ye therefore the Lord of the harvest, that he will send forth labourers into his harvest. (Matt. 9:37-38)

Heal the sick, cleanse the lepers, raise the dead, cast out devils: freely ye have received, freely give. (Matt. 10:8)

Come unto me, all ye that labour and are heavy laden, and I will give you rest. Take my yoke upon you, and learn of me; for I am meek and lowly in heart: and ye shall find rest unto your souls. For my yoke is easy, and my burden is light. (Matt. 11:28-30)

Well done, thou good and faithful servant: thou hast been faithful over a few things, I will make thee ruler over many things: enter thou into the joy of thy lord. (Matt. 25:21)

Go ye therefore, and teach all nations, baptizing them in the name of the Father, and of the Son, and of the Holy Ghost: Teaching them to observe all things whatsoever I have commanded you: and, lo, I am with you alway, even unto the end of the world. (Matt. 28:19-20)

Suffer little children to come unto me, and forbid them not: for of such is the kingdom of God. (Luke 18:16)

By this shall all men know that ye are my disciples, if ye have love one to another. (John 13:35)

And daily in the temple, and in every house, they ceased not to teach and preach Jesus Christ. (Acts 5:42)

And we know that all things work together for good to them that love God. (Rom. 8:28)

Let love be without dissimulation. Abhor that which is evil; cleave to that which is good. (Rom. 12:9)

Be kindly affectioned one to another with brotherly love; in honour preferring one another. (Rom. 12:10)